NY TANTARAN'NY TAREHIMARIKA

THE NUMBER STORY

SMALL BOOK ONE

ENGLISH - MALAGASY

*Numbers Teach Children
Their Number Names*

written and illustrated by

MISS ANNA

Early Reader Edition of *The Number Story 1*
Bronze Medal Winner, 2016 Wishing Shelf Book Award

Cover by | Lumpy Publishing
Layout by | Lumpy Publishing
Translated by Tefy R.
Coloring by Jieeun Woo and Maria Mirabella

Library of Congress Control Number: 2018902040

Names: Miss Anna, author.
Title: Number story : numbers teach children their number names / Miss Anna.
Description: Portland, OR: Lumpy Publishing, 2018.
Identifiers: ISBN 978-1-945977-72-5 | LCCN 2018902040
Summary: The pictures and rhymes present stories which introduce numbers 0-10.
Subjects: LCSH Numeration—English--Malagasy--Pictorial works--Juvenile literature. | BISAC JUVENILE NONFICTION /
Languages: English--Malagasy
Classification: LCC QA141.3 .M57 2018 | DDC 513—dc23

Publisher: Lumpy Publishing
Website: www.missannabooks.com
Email: missanna@missannabooks.com

Paperback: ISBN 978-1-945977-72-5
Printed in the U.S.A.   1 3 5 7 9 10 8 6 4 2

Te hianatra isa miaraka
aminay ve ianao?

It is very easy and a lot of fun!

Tsy sarotra sady mahafinaritra!

Say-along our little jingle

Hirao ary ity hira kely ity!

starting from Number One!

Handeha isika hanomboka amin'ny Iray!

1

ONE   looks like my one finger.

IRAY

Ohatrany fanondroko iray.

ONE!
'RAY!

2
TWO trails a tail.

ROA
Misy rambony.

A TAIL! RAMBO!

3

THREE has bumps.

TELO

Ohatrany havoana.

Jereo ireo havoana!

4

FOUR   carries a sail.

EFATRA

Mitondra lain-tsambo izy.

4
A SAIL!
LAIN-TSAMBO!

5

FIVE   is a racing track.

DIMY

Dia làlana hoan'ny fihazakazahana.

VROOM
VROUMM!
1

6

SIX curves like a snail.

ENINA

Miolana ohatrany sifotra.

A SNAIL! SIFOTRA!

7

SEVEN has a sharp angle.

FITO

Misy kiho maranitra.

OUCH!
KAY!

8

EIGHT   is rollercoaster rails.

VALO

Ohatrany *montagne russe*.

OUUAIIIIISS!
YIPPEE!

NINE is a bubble on a stick.

SIVY

Bulle ambony tehina kely io.

A BUBBLE!   BULLE!

10

TEN   is an eye of a whale.

FOLO

Mason-trozona izy io.

HELLO!
SALAMA Ô!

And
Ary

0

ZERO is an empty pail.

HAOTRA

Siny tsy feno.

IT'S EMPTY!
Foana le izy!

Thank you for playing with us today.

We had a lot of fun too!

Misaotra anao nilalao
niaraka aminay androany.
Faly izahay niara nihira taminao!

We are your Number friends,
Zero to Ten,
Who will be here for you~
Namanay koa ianao
haotra hatramin'ny folo!
Eo anilanao foana izahay~

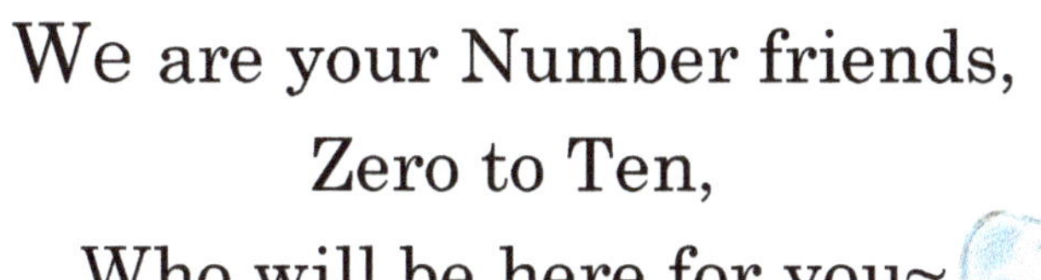

Bye-bye now!
See you again soon!
Veloma ary!
Mandrapihaona indray!

The Numbers are *SINGING* too!

To sing-a-long, look for Miss Anna Number Story
at your favorite music store like iTUNES.

MP3

Numbers 0-10
IDENTIFYING
& COUNTING

Numbers 11-20
& Ordinals

first, second, third...

Numbers 0-100
& Place Values

ones, tens, hundreds...

About Clocks
& Telling Time

hours, minutes, seconds

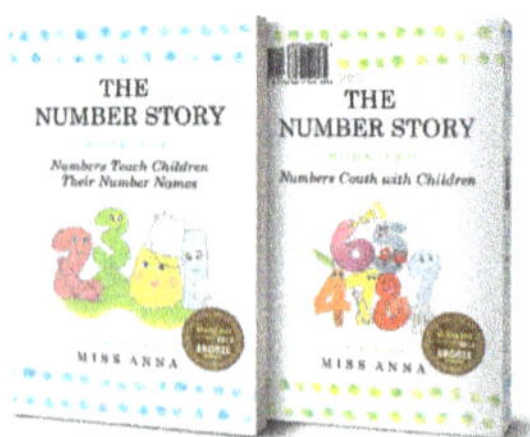

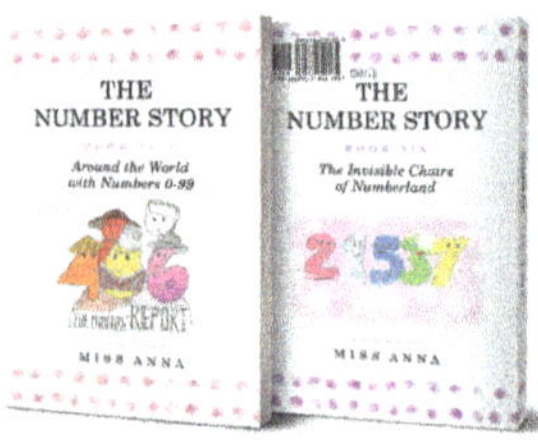

Number Story 1 & 2

isbn: 978-0-996216-48-7

Number Story 3 & 4

isbn: 978-1-945977-01-5

Number Story 5 & 6

isbn: 978-1-945977-06-0

Number Story 7 & 8

isbn: 978-1-949320-40-4

For more Miss Anna books to love,
visit us at

www.missannabooks.com

Numbers are working hard all over the world!
Come Travel the World with Us!

www.ingramcontent.com/pod-product-compliance
Lightning Source LLC
Chambersburg PA
CBHW040859070726
47599CB00035B/2229